# BUILDING HIGH PERFORMANCE TEAMS

# Better Management Skills

This highly popular range of inexpensive paperbacks covers all areas of basic management. Practical, easy to read and instantly accessible, these guides will help managers to improve their business or communication skills. Those marked * are available on audio cassette.

The books in this series can be tailored to specific company requirements. For further details, please contact the publisher, Kogan Page, telephone 0171 278 0433, fax 0171 837 6348.

Be a Successful Supervisor
Be Positive
Business Creativity
Business Etiquette
Coaching Your Employees
Conducting Effective Interviews
Counselling Your Staff
Creative Decision-making
Creative Thinking in Business
Delegating for Results
Effective Employee Participation
Effective Meeting Skills
Effective Performance Appraisals*
Effective Presentation Skills
Empowerment
First Time Supervisor
Get Organised!
Goals and Goal Setting
How to Communicate Effectively*
How to Develop a Positive Attitude*
How to Develop Assertiveness
How the Manage Organisational Change
How to Motivate People*
How to Understand Financial Statements
How to Write a Staff Manual
Improving Employee Performance
Improving Relations at Work
Keeping Customers for Life
Leadership Skills for Women

Learning to Lead
Make Every Minute Count*
Making TQM Work
Managing Cultural Diversity at Work
Managing Disagreement Constructively
Managing Organisational Change
Managing Part-time Employees
Managing Quality Customer Service
Managing Your Boss
Marketing for Success
Memory Skills in Business
Office Management
Personnel Testing
Productive Planning
Project Management
Quality Customer Service
Rate Your Skills as a Manager
Sales Training Basics
Self-managing Teams
Selling Professionally
Successful Negotiation
Successful Presentation Skills
Successful Telephone Techniques
Systematic Problem-solving and Decision-making
Team Building
Training Methods that Work
The Woman Manager

# BUILDING HIGH PERFORMANCE TEAMS

Sandy Pokras

KOGAN
PAGE

First published in the United States of America in 1995 entitled *Rapid Team Deployment* by Crisp Publications Inc, 1200 Hamilton Court, Menlo Park, CA 94025, USA.

This edition first published in Great Britain in 1996 by Kogan Page Ltd, 120 Pentonville Road, London N1 9JN

Reprinted 1998

---

**British Library Cataloguing in Publication Data**

A CIP record for this book is available from the British Library.

ISBN 0 7494 1906 7

---

Typeset by BookEns Ltd., Royston, Herts.
Printed and bound in Great Britain by Clays Ltd, St Ives plc.

# Contents

# Introduction

*Building High Performance Teams* focuses on teams with a definite lifecycle rather than self-directed natural work groups or management teams whose missions never end. This leaves a lot of territory. We'll talk about groups with short assignments as well as projects that take months or even years to complete. And we'll consider cross-functional teams as well as those wholly within your unit. Rapid team deployment (RTD) works with teams dedicated to:

- Implementation or discrete tasks
- Problem-solving or corrective action
- Statistical process control
- Business process re-engineering
- New process development
- Quality or continuous improvement
- Employee involvement
- Benchmarking
- New product design and manufacture
- Concurrent engineering.

You'll probably find other examples within your organisation. Frankly, the names don't count. The mechanics we'll cover apply equally well, regardless of the mission of the team you want to improve. Although we won't discuss permanent teams, many of the tools that follow are necessary and vital to self-directed work teams.

# CHAPTER 1
# Defining Team Direction

## Team mechanics

Many people think of a team as a task force, which is a temporary grouping of individuals asked to assist an accountable person in carrying out a specific assignment. When you need cross-functional expertise, a task force can work. But if only one person is accountable, we're not talking true teamwork and trend-setting accomplishments.

For others, a team is a committee, a continuing meeting of parties chosen to consider a specific subject and make recommendations, but typically without authority to act. A committee's updates, information transfers and exploratory discussions can be valuable, but teamwork implies ownership and commitment.

### Team definition
Here's the definition of a team we're striving to achieve. A team is a group of willing and trained individuals who are:

- United around a common goal
- Depending on each other to achieve it
- Structured to work together
- Sharing responsibility for their task
- Empowered to implement decisions.

7

Team members can't be ordered; they must be willing. A team's unity stems from the challenging goal the members accept. They share responsibility, authority and accountability because they can't get their job done alone. They decide by consensus, which means everyone agrees and no one loses when they differ. They have power to implement decisions, because without it, they probably won't do a very good job.

*Exercise*
### High-performance teamwork
Think about the teams you've been involved with. Did any of them operate well? This book will show you how to build the following 13 characteristics of a high-performance unit. Use this list to plan team-building, measure a team's performance level or decide how much time you have for team development. Measure performance on a scale of 1 to 10, with 1 being poor, 5 being average, and 10 being excellent.

| Characteristic | Description | Rating |
|---|---|---|
| 1. **Purpose** | A clear, challenging and inspiring common purpose | |
| 2. **Membership** | Complete, willing, skilled, available and trained membership | |
| 3. **Leadership** | Principled leadership with high standards to build the team and guide results until the team takes charge | |
| 4. **Structure** | A flexible, defined, results-oriented structure of roles, processes and procedures under team control | |
| 5. **Plans** | Long- and short-range plans based on a team roadmap with measurable milestones | |
| 6. **Participation** | Active participation of all team members who follow through | |
| 7. **Communication** | Open communication and informed members | |
| 8. **Trust** | Mutual trust, support and | |

|  |  |  |
|---|---|---|
|  | collaboration so that team-mates support one another | _____ |
| 9. Consensus | Critical decisions by consensus, especially when differences produce conflict | _____ |
| 10. Ownership | Joint ownership, entrepreneurial spirit and shared responsibility for implementation | _____ |
| 11. Synergy | Active cooperation between team members | _____ |
| 12. Recognition | Appropriate rewards, frequent recognition and routine celebrations | _____ |
| 13. Empowerment | Sufficient empowerment to enable the team to achieve its mission | _____ |

# Stages of team development

High performance, or any team performance at all, is not instant nor automatic. Groups have development stages.

No matter how skilled you are at launching teams or how experienced their members are, *forming groups* tend to act shy, tentative and uncertain. They might even be anxious and suspicious. There's not a lot of energy, investment or work accomplished very quickly. This forming stage is often frustrating for task-oriented managers who want instant results and don't know how to accelerate this process. This is where all teams start off.

If you succeed at building interest and commitment to work together, your reward is storming. *Storming teams* are much more open, but not usually very positive. They tend to complain, criticise and disagree. The good news is that they're getting involved and communicating, although it's not yet the kind of team spirit you'd hoped for. Team-builders who don't know how to facilitate storming can decide that teams are ineffective and disband them before they have a chance to accomplish anything.

*Norming teams* shift their attention from internal tensions to their work challenge. As they resolve their differences, relationships improve. They can express themselves positively even when they have problems. Norming teams don't have all the answers, but they make steady process in learning how to tackle their job. At last, you're probably thinking, this is what you wanted in the first place.

*Performing teams* rate high on all 13 characteristics of the team performance rating form (page 8). These people aren't just getting the job done, they're totally committed, coordinated and cooperative. They are a self-regulating, self-sufficient and self-directed unit, and nothing can stop them achieving their purpose. Obviously, it takes time and work to arrive here. The more skilled the team-building approach, the more rapid the team's ultimate deployment.

When your high-performance team accomplishes its purpose, you'll face another problem: adjourning. Performing teams don't want to break up, and maybe they shouldn't. You've got to do something with all this excitement and ability — either recharter this group or use the team members as the nucleus of new projects. Otherwise you'll have trouble recruiting teams in the future.

### Team performance accelerators

You can't create a high-performance team by edict. It takes action and effort. We shall explore three sets of proven tools for team development: defining roles, planning the team's work and maximising participation. The following chart introduces the tools and structures that accelerate team operations.

---

**Role definition**

| | |
|---|---|
| **Leaders** | *Team sponsor.* The manager who owns the team's territory and champions its work. <br> *Team facilitator.* Group process expert assigned to coach, train and guide the team. <br> *Team leader.* Elected or appointed team member who builds the team. |

---

| | |
|---|---|
| **Members** | *Team members.* Active owners who collect data, decide jointly, assign action and report. |

*Meeting hats.* Rotating assignments that keep meetings functioning efficiently.
*Work functions.* Skills specialities inherited or developed to implement team decisions.

| Planning tools | |
|---|---|
| **Charter** | Statement of the team's mission, challenge and mechanics serving as common goal and contract. |
| **Roadmap** | Measurable objectives defining what the team will deliver according to a master plan. |
| **Public relations** | Targets and actions to ensure that customers, suppliers and stakeholders work with the team. |

| Participation tools | |
|---|---|
| **Meeting tools** | Agendas, discussion moderation and process reviews. |
| **Ground rules** | Values established by a team to guide behaviour. |
| **Brainstorming** | Quick, creative idea generation without judgement or evaluation. |
| **Data analysis** | Input, research, data collection and experiments so that decisions are based on facts. |
| **Consensus** | Joint decisions that merge opinions, resolve conflict, satisfy all needs and are supported. |

# To team or not to team?

Before you launch a team, decide why you're doing it and why it's a good idea. When a team's purpose is clear, you can plan and organise the effort so that minimum time and effort are wasted. You'll be able to brief the team better so it can hit the ground running.

### Team goals
There are seven reasons you might want to launch a team:

1. **Results**. Increasing output and productivity or improving service and quality.
2. **Efficiency**. Lowering costs, reducing cycle time, eliminating waste and solving problems.

3. **Synergy**. Combining brainpower and increasing creativity by getting different disciplines to work together.
4. **Working relationships**. Improving communication, co-operation and consensus.
5. **Attitudes**. Improving morale, job satisfaction and the willingness to raise performance standards.
6. **Empowerment**. Involving workers in decisions, increasing span of control and raising everyone's sense of responsibility.
7. **Cross-functional work**. Confronting cross-departmental issues and multidisciplinary problems using outside resources and expertise.

## Team costs

You have decided you want to accomplish one or more of the above goals. Before continuing with RTD, consider alternatives. You could:

- Do the work yourself
- Ignore the issue and hope it goes away
- Delegate to a qualified individual
- Form a task force under an accountable person's control
- Escalate to higher management
- Hire a consultant
- Charter a high-performance team.

A high-performance team offers the best long-term benefits, but it takes work and time (weeks or months) to build a team to top performance. To decide how much team-building you'll invest in, first consider the resources, support and obstacle resolution needed. When you launch a team, you're really committing to provide:

- **Labour.** Part of teamwork is work away from production, also requiring skilled team leadership, expert technical support and team facilitation.
- **Time investment.** Team members need time for meetings, data collection, outside preparation, coaching sessions and documentation.
- **Lead time.** Teams need time for members to move up their

learning curves and the overall team to learn to work together before they get results.

- **Management input.** The team's manager needs to brief, train, guide, monitor and stay in touch to keep the team informed.
- **Management support.** Management needs to give up some direct control and concentrate on providing rewards and recognition.
- **Relationships.** Teams need training as a group, opportunities for face-to-face communication and conflict resolution skills.
- **Obstacle resolution.** Expect to meet resistance to change, reluctance to share information, distrust, insecurity and unwillingness to take risks.

### Cost/benefit analysis

Is the cost worth the potential benefit of starting a team? Ask yourself if you have time for the necessary meetings, training, planning, supporting, coaching and troubleshooting. If you can invest in team-building now, plan big and hope for huge rewards later. If you need quick results with untrained people, scale back your expectations. Too many managers announce that they're forming a high-performance, totally empowered team before they consider costs. After starting the process, they back out. As a result, many teams start at a crawl and then slow down because of insufficient resources.

# Empowerment

To empower means to give official authority, delegate legal power or give faculties or abilities to enable. In the illustration overleaf, just outside the bull's-eye, the second ring is the target of empowered teamwork. The ring of barriers shows what's in the way.

### How to empower and enable

Empowerment isn't absolute. Teamwork means sharing power. Your job is to define what the team will be responsible for, their authority, and what management's role will be. The cost

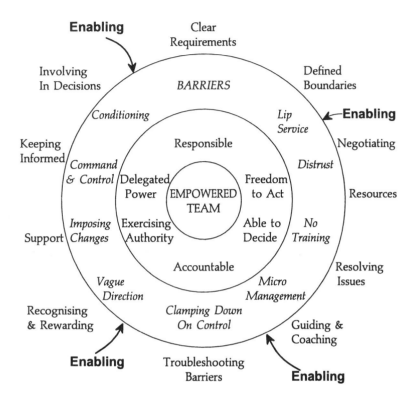

of empowerment is clearly communicating goals, requirements and boundaries from the start.

Empowering a team is challenging, and doing RTD is more so. Employees are conditioned to receiving direction. How can you direct them to be productive without outside direction? How can you enable them to accomplish things that others haven't?

Empowerment really means:

- Giving workers authority, influence and control over their own destiny
- Involving people in decisions that affect them
- Creating ownership and commitment to their team charter
- Allowing them the freedom to implement their own decisions
- Making them responsible and holding them accountable

- Helping them to find their own way out of conflict instead of clamping down.

Lip service alone won't do much to empower a team. Teams must be enabled to achieve their mission by your:

- Giving clear general direction without being over-prescriptive
- Negotiating instead of imposing a team charter
- Providing training and support to develop potential
- Giving time, tools, money, space and equipment
- Helping them to consider new options when they make hard choices
- Removing barriers and troubleshooting problems they can't control
- Rewarding initiative, innovation, cooperation and risk taking.

**Planning empowerment level**
A valuable team-launching exercise is to plan what you want them involved in before they start. Use the Team Empowerment Worksheet shown overleaf to plan what teams should work on now and what you hope they get to in the future. (Note the blank lines at the bottom for activities peculiar to a specific team.)

## *Team Empowerment Worksheet*

| Team activity | Now | Future |
|---|---|---|
| 1. Membership selection | | |
| 2. Team charter development | | |
| 3. Team project plan | | |
| 4. Team budget | | |
| 5. Training plans | | |
| 6. Meeting schedule | | |
| 7. Meeting agendas | | |
| 8. Meeting evaluation | | |
| 9. Problem analysis | | |
| 10. Solution decision | | |
| 11. Selling team proposals | | |
| 12. Implementation control | | |
| 13. Procedure documentation | | |
| 14. Performance review | | |
| 15. Team rewards | | |
| 16. Measurement of results | | |
| 17. Communication | | |
| 18. | | |
| 19. | | |
| 20. | | |

*Exercise*
## Case study team selection
It's time for you to choose a real situation to use throughout this book to apply the tools and principles presented.

1. Review the reasons teams are formed (team goals from page 11) and then decide which are needed in your organisation. List these goals on the left side of the Cost/ Benefit Analysis Worksheet.
2. Calculate what you'll have to invest to achieve these goals using teamwork (team costs from page 12) and list them on the right side of the worksheet.
3. Consider which situations seem like a good investment. Which do you believe warrant team-building? Which would serve as a good learning example as well?
4. Select one example to serve as your case study team. Decide firmly, since we'll delve into this case study. Record your choice at the bottom of the worksheet.

### *Cost/Benefit Analysis Worksheet*

| Benefits of teamwork desired | Costs of deploying this team |
|---|---|
| | |
| **Case study team** | |

# Rapid team deployment

Few three-month project teams ever reach high performance and total self-sufficiency. Members can't spend six weeks getting ready. Neither do you want them to storm for weeks, throw away most of their resources and then slap together a last-minute proposal that no one wants to implement anyway. That's not the idea of RTD, but their project can still benefit from cooperation, collaboration and synergy.

You might have the best intentions in the world when you announce you're forming an empowered self-directed team. But consider:

- Do you want the team to rework the basic processes you use to produce your product or service?
- Will the team be ready right away to work directly with your customers?
- Do you want the team to dictate what to say to your senior management?
- Will you give them full budget control?
- If you can't answer 'Yes' right now, when will you be able to?

If you have any hesitation in answering these questions, don't make claims you won't substantiate. Don't call the team empowered, because they'll think that's absolute. Don't tell them they're self-directed if you ever intend to redirect their efforts when you or your boss become dissatisfied. Don't tell them to do what they think is best if you might ever respond, 'That's not what I wanted you to do.'

**Our theme**

The theme of RTD is simple: Build and empower the team to the degree possible for the time you're willing to invest in team development. Define the task and its boundaries, organise the team accordingly and give them only essential tools. RTD is all about getting a group to rise to the occasion by concentrating narrowly.

Realise there's a business equation at work. Make your

calculations wisely and stay the course. Decide which team-building tools will help you to achieve your purpose. Be realistic about natural growth cycles, and don't initiate a team unless the situation warrants the investment. If it doesn't, find another means to get the job done.

Here are two examples:

1. You're launching a two-year project team to introduce a new service, you've got time for natural team growth. You'll want to invest in all the high-performance components you can to help you get the most out of this vital team. Let them spend more time on planning. Send them off to work on it. Give them access to lots of experts. Encourage them to use experimental personality-style surveys. Feed them all sorts of information and regular updates. Be patient with their internal struggles. You can make the case that team-building will pay in the long run.

2. You've got a three-month project and must choose the tools that fit that situation. Give your team more specific directions, established checkpoints and defined resources. Make their initial training more focused. Watch them closely and keep reminding them of their challenge, but don't distract them with irrelevant information or micro-management. With the right support, expect that they'll build to an adequate level of performance. They don't have the time to grow into a world-class model in a few weeks, so don't encourage them to spend much time on longer-term concerns. Help them to confront their urgent task now.

**How to do it**

To deploy a project team as quickly as possible with the highest chance of success and maximum synergy, you – the team's manager – need a game plan. What exactly do you want the team to accomplish? Who needs to be involved? How much empowerment do you want to give them? What information do they need and how will you get it to them? How much time can you all invest in developing teamwork?

How will you stay in touch without smothering them? What will you do to support them and shun interference?

Then you need to give them the right amount of time, information and resources for their project. Guide them to plan, define roles and build participation at the right depth for their task. RTD will give you the entire formula for building the highest performance level possible.

## The team environment

If everyone in your organisation was skilled and experienced at sponsoring, leading, facilitating and participating in high-performance teams, teams could be deployed much faster. The army uses this rapid-deployment-force model to prepare for all contingencies. To build a universal team environment:

- Train all management levels, functional groups and employee disciplines in high-performance teamwork
- Launch narrowly focused demonstration projects that let newcomers learn and practise
- Staff a team support unit to plan and conduct training, troubleshoot problems and make available proven team processes
- Maintain an up-to-date database of training, assignments and experience
- Rotate everyone into different team roles to build depth
- Regulate team commitments so that a pool of qualified team members is always available for rapid deployment and no one is overcommitted.

Though these efforts are most conducive to long-term team efforts, they may not be the ideal place for you to start using RTD.

# Defining team requirements

### Team lifecycle

By making it this far, you've decided teamwork is warranted for your project and will be worth the investment. Now your challenge will be to guide the new team through the team lifecycle.

This flowchart says that you first must give the project a clear sense of direction, get the group recruited and organised, invest time and effort in team-building to fuse individuals into a cohesive unit and then let them demonstrate effective teamwork that won't be perfect so you'll use continuous improvement until they have to disperse. This description defines the agenda we'll follow to present RTD.

### Team direction

Before you can form a team, you'll need to brief potential members on the organisation's critical business need, its overall strategy and where their goals fit in. Without clear objectives, it is nearly impossible to recruit skilled and committed members.

Too wide a scope is a common mistake that slows teams down. Yet most of us tend to dump all sorts of elaborate demands on an untested group and then get angry when it flounders. We should know better. Err on the side of narrow requirements. Give a new team a chance for small wins before you expect it to conquer the world.

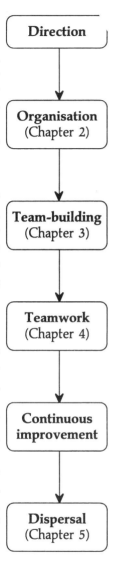

## Requirement techniques
Let's review three techniques for defining team requirements.

| Technique | Definition |
|---|---|
| **1.** Mission statement | → The team's purpose |
| **2.** Customer requirements | → What the customer expects |
| **3.** Team deliverables | → Measurable end products |

You need to use one or all of these methods to clarify what you want the team to be accountable for. Teamwork requires clear goal-setting, since the message must be communicated to different people from diverse backgrounds. Your aim is to unify the new group around these requirements once communicated.

Here's the rub. Define the requirements too thoroughly and you disempower the team. Define the requirements too vaguely and the team flounders. You're looking for the right balance. Draft your best requirement statements and be prepared to negotiate once team members form their own opinions.

*1. Mission statement*
A mission statement should briefly define the team's customer and the customer's need, what product or service the team must deliver to meet the need and how the team should deliver that product or service.

Organisational missions typically aren't measurable. Instead, a mission statement defines why the team is formed, what it exists for and where it should head. By suggesting a general mission statement, you can define direction now and remain open enough to negotiate exact accountability later.

*2. Customer requirements*
Another way to define the team's requirements is by using the customer–supplier chain as this diagram shows.

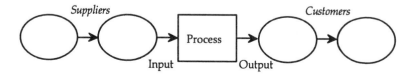

Here's what these symbols stand for.

**Input**  What you need to get your job done.

**Suppliers**  People, functions and departments (internal and external) from whom you receive inputs.

**Process**  The sequence of actions that constitutes your job function.

**Output**  The products that you create.

**Customers**  People, functions and departments (internal and external) who consume (receive, utilise, value and benefit from) your outputs.

Use the Customer Requirement Worksheet as a guide to this technique. If you start by determining what outputs or services you expect from the team, you can discover who consumes those outputs. By asking these internal or external customers how they will judge successful results, you can define specific requirements for the team. Typically, these take the form of satisfaction factors such as volume, quality, cycle time, prompt delivery or other specifications.

### *Customer Requirement Worksheet*

| Outputs | Customers | Requirements |
|---------|-----------|--------------|
|         |           |              |
|         |           |              |
|         |           |              |
|         |           |              |
|         |           |              |
|         |           |              |
|         |           |              |
|         |           |              |

The strategic planning team's mission statement specifies an output, a business plan. They use this worksheet to define categories of customers and what they would each like to see in a business plan. Top management want a short executive summary with conclusions supported by data and analysis. The engineers want everything presented in flowcharts. Manufacturing employees want simple statements of how their operations would change. From these deliberations, the team plan the best format for the document.

### 3. Team deliverables
'Deliverable' means a measurable product or output that is completed and turned over to the customer.

Use these questions to define team deliverables.

1. What output does the team need to deliver?
2. What outcome is expected from the project?
3. What final product will be valuable to the customer?
4. What are the customer's requirements?
5. How will the customer decide acceptability?
6. What major milestones must be met?
7. What long-, medium- and short-term objectives are established?
8. What are the project's deadlines?
9. How will the team sponsor measure success?
10. What continuing product or service is desired?

Even if mission statements and customer requirements aren't measurable enough for short-term accountability, deliverables must be. Deliverables are best defined as SMART objectives:

**S**pecific
**M**easurable
**A**greed
**R**esult-oriented
**T**imed

Record your answers to the 10 questions above on the SMART Worksheet to complete this method of defining requirements.

## SMART Worksheet

| |
|---|
| **Accomplishment:** *What do you want the team to achieve?* |
| **Specific.** *What do you want them to accomplish?* |
| **Measurable.** *How will you monitor progress?* |
| **Agreed.** *How will this deliverable satisfy each team member's needs?* |
| **Result.** *What is the finished product or final outcome?* |
| **Time.** *How long will it take to complete?* |
| **Deliverable.** *Rewrite the deliverable to include all the above.* |

*Exercise*
**Team requirements**
Let's use these direction-setting tools to define requirements for your case study team.

**1.** Decide if one, two or all three of the techniques presented will best guide you in forming and recruiting the team.
**2.** Work through the worksheets you choose.
**3.** Rewrite the results overleaf.

*Your case study team requirements worksheet*

_____

_____

_____

_____

_____

_____

_____

# Management support roles

If you've been able to work through the exercises so far, you're probably the team's sponsor. A team sponsor is typically the manager who:

- Is responsible for the team's problem or process
- Is primarily responsible to a customer for a product or service
- Controls the territory's resources by role or by delegation
- Chooses to seek solutions or improvements through teamwork
- Has the authority to approve or reject team recommendations
- Champions the team.

### Team sponsor functions
An effective team sponsor initiates and supports a team by:

- Providing direction and guidance
- Negotiating the team charter
- Authorising time and resources
- Coaching the team leader
- Staying in touch and monitoring progress
- Holding the team accountable
- Committing to follow through and promote team success
- Supporting whatever the team decides to implement

- Clearing roadblocks and removing barriers
- Recognising and rewarding team accomplishments.

To do this, a team sponsor has seven distinct functions.

*1. Direction*
Clarify higher management goals and organisation needs, brief the team, present requirements and boundaries and define authority and empowerment levels.

*2. Enabling*
Provide adequate tools, training and resources; authorise ample team-member work time; permit team development; allow the team decision-making authority and don't impose unrealistic time constraints.

*3. Support*
Honour team needs and desires by being open to changes and being willing to negotiate and take risks the team thinks are necessary, and by expecting to approve and implement what the team proposes.

*4. Guidance*
Monitor team progress and problems; encourage small, quick wins to build confidence; advise, coach and support instead of demanding and directing and keep the team informed.

*5. Follow-through*
Read team minutes, meet team leaders, occasionally attend team meetings, respond to team questions, receive presentations positively, be consistent with commitments.

*6. Remove barriers*
Accept setbacks without overreacting; outlaw interference, remove obstacles and clear roadblocks; let the team handle problems when appropriate.

*7. Champion the team*
Serve as the team's management liaison, advocate team solutions, reward and acknowledge team efforts and participate in team celebrations.

If this looks like a lot of work, it is. Eventually a high-performance team will relieve you of much of this work, but it doesn't happen instantly or automatically. You're committing to these seven sponsor functions in return for the team committing to achieve their charter. That takes work from everyone.

### Task vs team focus
One of the many choices a team sponsor has to make is whether to emphasise task results or team building.

Ideally, you want both, but by starting any team-building at all, you're accepting the challenge of balancing time for project work against team development. When the balance is off, these consequences might occur.

| Examples of too much TASK focus | Possible consequences |
|---|---|
| • Total focus on work and task by the project manager<br>• Pushing the team for results members are not ready to produce<br>• Too much pressure on deadlines and efficiency | • Some team members remain uncomfortable<br><br>• Conflicts are ignored and creativity suffers<br><br>• Dominators run meeting with little participation from others |
| Examples of too much TEAM focus | Possible consequences |
| • Personal problems absorb a lot of team meeting time<br><br>• Team meetings become non-stop gripe sessions<br><br>• Frequent blocked consensus stalls team progress | • The team makes very little progress on its project<br>• Action items never get done without repercussions<br>• Deadlines are ignored and checkpoints are missed |

**Top 10 team sponsor guidelines**

1. Charter teams you intend to support and no others. When you empower a team, consider that providing adequate information, resources, training, time, guidance and support is a moral obligation.

2. Clarify your expectations, boundaries and performance standards when you start. Guide, update and reinforce teams so you never have to say no.

3. Be assertive about what you need and want from teams, but be willing to negotiate about how they want to proceed.

4. Keep teams informed and let them know how they're doing, but don't micromanage.

5. Attend occasional team meetings when invited or for scheduled agenda items, honouring their ground rules and meeting mechanics. Avoid vague or conflicting feedback to individual team members about public team business.

6. Hold teams accountable but recognise their achievements too. Uphold agreements with teams and don't change priorities midstream unless unexpected developments warrant it.

7. Build mutual trust by treating team members as equals and avoiding intimidation tactics. Encourage openness about problems by coaching, not punishing.

8. Don't make unilateral decisions when teams can decide. Avoid knee-jerk reactions when teams may be able to self-correct on their own.

9. Whenever possible, say yes and take swift action on team proposals, or advise on adjustments needed to win approval.

10. Report team progress and proposals to upper management with pride, giving them full credit, total support and deserved recognition.

**Upper management's impact on teamwork**

Even if you sign up wholeheartedly for the demanding job of team sponsor, your team may still run into management support problems that slow teamwork immeasurably. What if:

- Cross-functional bosses won't let their members attend meetings?
- Other units won't cooperate because of other priorities?
- Your team's work adds to others' stress?
- Needed resources are under the control of uninvolved people?

It's easy to say that your job, team sponsor, is to champion the team and remove barriers. But what if upper management disagrees?

*Steering council function*
Teams deploy more rapidly and thrive more fully when overseen by a strong team steering council. A steering council is a model management team composed of team sponsors or their bosses who are responsible for planning and guiding how their organisation implements, applies and integrates team-work.

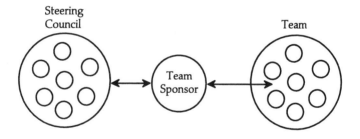

This diagram shows the team sponsor as the communication link between the steering council and the team. Whether team sponsors are members of the council or report directly to council members, they must represent consensus from above while guiding the team.

*Ideal world*
Ideally, a team steering council would:

- Establish vision, strategy and long-range plans
- Prioritise business issues that teams should address

- Authorise resources and coordinate training
- Oversee the chartering of teams by their members
- Develop and continuously improve the teamwork process
- Monitor team progress and troubleshoot problems
- Support team efforts and drive cross-functional cooperation
- Publicise results and deploy lessons learned
- Provide recognition and rewards.

If all your peers deploy high-performance teams, everyone's customers and suppliers will understand and cooperate. Your bosses will back you up. Your marketing department will praise you. Your end users will crave your improved quality.

What if you don't live in an ideal world? Without a steering council, it seems you're committed to taking on some of their functions on your own. You need to enlist your boss, his or her peers and upper management to support your team.

Although this sounds like a daunting task at first, think about what you'll do if your team hits a political wall midway through the project. Smoothing the path for the team may, in the long run, turn out to be relatively cost-effective insurance.

*Exercise*
**Management support roles**
Let's apply what we've covered to your case study team.

1. Who is the best choice for case study team sponsor? You? Someone above or below you in the hierarchy?

_____

2. Why? List the qualifications of your recommended team sponsor from the role definition and functions on page 27 to back up your choice.

_____

_____

3. Which management team already fulfils the functions as your case study team's steering council?

_____

4. If none, list the managers whose understanding, involvement and support are needed for the case study team to succeed.

_____

_____

5. How will you secure support from these managers and protect the team to ensure it can flourish in as positive an environment as possible?

_____

_____

## Establishing team leadership

Leading is different from managing. Leading means to show the way by going first and guiding direction by persuasion. Managing implies command and control. Leaders concentrate on getting others to learn, grow and win. Managers concentrate on getting results because their bosses expect it. We all know there's a time for both leading and managing, but the stark truth is that leading a team effectively in the short run produces both growth and results in the long run. Command and control may get immediate results, but unfortunately only the manager, not the team, is motivated for the next assignment.

So when we talk about a team leader, we mean an elected or appointed team member who builds the team and guides joint action on its work: not an authority figure or a supervisor, but a team member who has a unique function. Some of the characteristics frequently reported of good leaders are:

- Visionary
- Dedicated
- Communicative
- Good Listener
- Coach
- Role Model

- Dependable
- Objective
- Positive
- Open
- Involving
- Initiator

## Team leader functions

A team leader initially inherits five functions when accepting the role:

### 1. Team builder
Assess team health, plan training, unify the group, build team spirit and mutual trust, resolve conflicts and adjust membership if necessary.

### 2. Team members' coach
Meet all members individually, motivate, reinforce positive behaviour, give advice and induct new members.

### 3. Work coordinator
Clarify sponsor goals, help to complete plans, ensure roles are filled, guide data collection, keep team on track and troubleshoot problems.

### 4. Meeting chair
Plan, organise and chair meetings; ensure public recording of ideas; facilitate team consensus; assign action items and distribute minutes.

### 5. Public relations organiser
Identify stakeholders, assign team representatives, plan reporting, coordinate contacts, solicit input and feedback and conduct presentations.

Since good team leaders are dedicated to working themselves out of a job, their attention is always on delegating. The sooner team members can take over these tasks, the higher the performance level of the team. In a truly world-class team, the team leader is merely a figurehead, since leadership is distributed, shared and rotated to whoever is best qualified for a specific function.

## Team leader selection

Team sponsors can appoint whoever they think would serve as the best team leader or let the team choose.

The method you choose depends on how urgent the task is and how high your confidence is in the team process. For a shorter project, you might pick whoever can build the team to get results quickest. For a long-term team, you might lean towards the elected leader. Either way, base the choice of leader both on technical knowledge and interpersonal skill. If you're resisting the elected method because you think the team will make their choice for the wrong reasons, give members a balanced list of selection criteria so it's not a popularity contest or a long political campaign.

You might want to consider appointing a team leader pro tem for several months. Select a temporary leader who doesn't want the glory and announces at the start that he or she will give up the responsibility later. A team that's around long enough can choose a more permanent leader when members know better what the job demands.

## Team facilitator

A team facilitator is the group process consultant who coaches the team leader, advises the team sponsor on team dynamics and trains the team to use team methods and improvement tools.

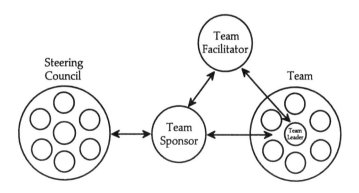

It doesn't matter much whether you recruit a team facilitator who is full time (handling six to ten teams), part time (10–20 per cent of their time), or an outside consultant. What matters to the speed of team results is that the team facilitator is trained in group dynamics and team tools, attends all team meetings, meets the team leader frequently and:

- Observes
- Advises
- Responds
- Explains
- Helps
- Guides
- Coaches
- Encourages

- Trains
- Models
- Mentors
- Demonstrates
- Delegates
- Wears hats only temporarily
- Works through the team leader
- Remains neutral and objective

The best team facilitators don't:

- Work in the chain of command under which the team operates
- Contribute technical expertise
- Act as an actual team member
- Give project opinions or discuss content areas
- Decide for the team
- Meet team members individually unless requested
- Run the team's project.

When you recruit a team facilitator, look for someone with an impartial attitude who communicates well, understands group dynamics, runs effective meetings, gives constructive feedback and builds people's self-confidence.

**Team facilitator functions**
The specific functions of a team facilitator include:

- **Team trainer.** Help assess training needs, create development plans, identify outside resources, conduct workshops and provide just-in-time training.
- **Team leader's coach.** Meet before and after each team meeting to debrief, reinforce, advise, troubleshoot and plan for improvements in future meetings.
- **Team-building guide.** Suggest team-building actions,

demonstrate new tools, clarify mechanics, facilitate initial discussions and mediate differences if asked.

- **Team process consultant.** Observe group dynamics, give feedback, encourage self-monitoring, advise about long-term growth and intervene only if essential.

*Exercise*
**Team leadership**
Let's apply what we've covered to your case study team.

**1.** What are the most important criteria for your leader?

_____

_____

**2.** Will you appoint the case study team leader or would it be best for the team to select their own?

_____

_____

**3.** If an appointment, who would you select?

_____

_____

**4.** Who will you try to recruit to serve as case study team facilitator?

_____

_____

**5.** What skills and expertise qualify this person as team facilitator?

_____

_____

# CHAPTER 2
# Organising Your Team

## Team recruitment

We've defined the support and leadership roles that a team needs, but what about our real target? A team member is an active participant who has a stake in the team's mission, shares responsibility for the team's work, conducts experiments and gathers data before team meetings, contributes information during meetings and represents the team to customers and co-workers. Teams report that they desire team members who are:

- Knowledgeable
- Committed
- Dependable
- Vocal, open, honest
- Involved
- Supportive

- Cooperative
- Good listeners
- Trusting
- Hard workers
- Flexible
- Enthusiastic.

Team members need to:

- **Share the team's work.** Contribute to team charter and plans, share responsibility, perform their roles, follow the plan and help to solve problems.
- **Represent the team.** Keep outsiders informed, make frequent contacts, collect customer input and participate in presentations.

- **Prepare to contribute.** Get trained, read minutes, complete action items, gather information, meet the team leader and be ready for meetings.
- **Participate in meetings.** Attend all meetings on time, participate fully, offer special expertise, listen, communicate openly, follow ground rules and work for consensus.

### Team member selection

It's important to choose the right team members. The Team Selection Flowchart can help.

Start with a clear mission statement so you know what you want the team to accomplish. Establish key qualifications and characteristics for team personnel. Selection criteria come in three S categories:

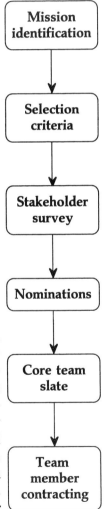

- **Skill.** Job knowledge and technical expertise unique to a special discipline.
- **Style.** Personal approach, attitude, motivation, communication and group skills that affect trust, cooperation and compatibility.
- **Stake.** Vested interest or sense of ownership resulting from personal interest, job needs, work area pressures, management priorities or performance goals.

Now survey stakeholders to see who would make good team players. Stakeholders are those inside or outside the organisation who have a stake in the team's work. These people include internal and external customers and suppliers; anyone involved directly in the process under study; anyone affected indirectly by the problem or situation; managers with the power to veto team recommendations and those whose support, resources or approval are needed for implementation. This is a long list, but you will save time eventually if you find out now whom you need to influence later to implement team decisions.

Nominations for your team can come from internal advertising, steering council suggestions, stakeholder requests, functional manager offers, informal volunteering, self-nomination, work group elections and personal recruitment interviews. To ensure that participation is at least partially voluntary, talk to nominees and bosses early. Then you will know that they are available, interested and motivated.

If you do your homework, you'll have too many candidates to choose from. Narrow the list into a core team balanced by the three Ss. A core team – those who attend all meetings and make all decisions – functions better if it includes only six to eight members. Larger team discussions become unwieldy with slower team building and postponed work progress.

### Contracting team members
Few organisations make time for the final vital recruiting step, team member contracting. A contract means a social agreement in which people agree to do something for each other. Remember, the extraordinary effort that you're hoping to get from a high-performance team is voluntary. Support begins by asking if members want to join, showing what's in it for them, and then negotiating around their needs.

## Team charter

The members of the world's fastest teams have a sharp sense of direction and solid understanding of how their work relates to organisational goals. This understanding is achieved with a clear, written, agreed description of the team's mission and how it relates to organisational goals, including general direction, membership and empowerment. This charter serves as a contract of key team mechanics among team members and between them and the team sponsor.

A team charter should be a two-way document. It defines what the team commits to do for the team sponsor and what the team sponsor agrees to do in return. Charters are constructed from answers to the following questions. Use only those elements that help to unify team and sponsor.

## General direction
- **Background.** Why was the team formed (include business goals, earlier similar projects, process history and customer concerns)?
- **Mission.** What is the team's special assignment, role or function (define the need, system or process to be addressed and its scope and boundaries)?
- **Roadmap choice.** Which type of master plan is best for this mission?
- **Deliverables.** What outcome does the team sponsor or customer expect, how will they measure success, what are the preliminary and final deadlines?
- **Name.** What will the team call itself, specifying its function and primary geographical and departmental location?

## Membership
- **Stakeholders.** Which customers must the team satisfy, which suppliers must they depend on, which team member managers and co-workers need to support it and who can influence or veto the team's decisions?
- **Team member roles.** Who will serve as the core team, what initial roles will they play, who will meet which stakeholders, and who can the team call in to help temporarily?
- **Team sponsor role.** What will the manager commit to do for the team and what functions will the team sponsor perform during and between team meetings?

## Empowerment
- **Team duties.** What activities will the team be expected to carry out?
- **Authority level.** What power does the team have (include what they can directly control and what needs approval in what way)?

- **Resources.** What budget, supplies, staff time, training, space, equipment and facilities will the organisation allocate to the team?
- **Reporting.** What written reports, individual contacts, checkpoints, reviews and formal presentations will the team give to whom how often, and which will they receive from whom and when?
- **Rewards.** How will the team be rewarded, how will team members be recognised for their contributions and what rewards will happen at which milestones?

## Team charter development

Theoretically, it would be nice to clarify all charter components immediately. In the real world of pressures, deadlines and limited resources, that rarely happens. It's better if management limits its involvement to specifying the minimum sense of direction so the team can find its own solutions. Here's the suggested rapid team deployment (RTD) programme for developing a team charter.

- **Requirements.** Define initial requirements for the team. If a steering council exists, be sure the team's goals align with its business goals and priorities.
- **Recruitment.** Recruit a team facilitator and possibly a team leader. Work with them to recruit core team members.
- **Draft MRDC.** Draft critical parts of the team charter using the MRDC rule of thumb. Mission, Roadmap, and Deliverables are specific charter components. Include the fourth, Constraints, if you or the team's customer need to dictate any other boundaries, limits, deadlines or requirements.
- **Briefing.** Brief the core team on its requirements and your MRDC draft. Since information determines power, any other background you can give will help.
- **Chartering retreat.** Host a chartering retreat, including any basic training, during which members discuss, negotiate and complete the parts of the charter they deem important. (An intensive two- to three-day session provides the fastest team deployment.)

- **Negotiate.** Let the team present its proposed charter and agree to as much as you possibly can. Negotiate adjustments where essential, but be careful not to dampen their enthusiasm and sense of ownership.

A team charter should be both binding and flexible. Refer to it regularly as a living document, and adjust it when needed. Occasional charter review keeps the team's sense of purpose alive and its actions focused, and when major changes occur, it provides a simple basis for renegotiation.

# Briefing the team

The better you prepare any project, the faster you can expect to get it off the ground. This rule applies strongly to teams, especially new ones. What can you tell them at the outset that will accelerate their team-building? Some answers are obvious: mission, deliverables, background, rewards and other key charter components. Others may not be so obvious.

### How to brief the team
To empower a team quickly, you have to brief them fully at the outset and then keep them fully informed. Give members the background to understand the big picture, customer requirements and any relevant history.

Which of the following do you have information about and could brief the forming team about swiftly? Which do they need to know to make rapid progress? Which of these might they want to know about?

☐ Customer requirements
☐ Customer feedback and satisfaction
☐ Competitive pressures
☐ Problem symptoms
☐ Process behaviour
☐ Process history
☐ Production statistics
☐ Financial performance

☐ Time constraints
☐ Money limitations
☐ Union agreements
☐ Regulatory requirements
☐ Safety considerations
☐ Labour or overtime constraints
☐ Equipment/facility availability
☐ Technology development

☐ Stakeholder involvement ☐ Senior management vision
☐ Earlier similar projects ☐ Driving business needs
☐ Related current efforts ☐ Strategic goals and objectives

If you put a tick in each square, you're right!

For the swiftest team-building, put together a presentation based on these and then follow these disclosure guidelines.

| Recommended | Not recommended |
| --- | --- |
| Complete information | Secrets |
| Full background data | Delay bad news |
| Trust the team | Protect their feelings |
| Confidentiality ground rules | The need-to-know rule |
| Define boundaries | Leave direction fuzzy |
| Agree on resources (time, money, facilities, equipment, space) | Wait and see |
| Train the team to understand | Hide financial and political details |

## Roadmaps

Different kinds of teamwork require different approaches. Enter the team's roadmap. A roadmap tells a team how to get where it wants to go by providing a step-by-step master plan that outlines the best route to follow for that type of work. A roadmap lays out the important actions that similar previous teams used to achieve success. The right roadmap provides a tested method that ensures even first-time teams won't omit essential actions.

With a logical order for approaching their assignment defined in advance, a team can plan and act quickly. Roadmaps carve up overwhelming tasks into confrontable chunks, provide defined milestones, suggest tools and make it easier to hold teams accountable without too much stress. Additional benefits of using a team roadmap include:

- Prevents continual firefighting without long-term progress
- Provides a framework for easy reporting and recognition
- Allows easily understandable documents to preserve history.

The table below explains the most common categories of project teams from the simplest to the most complex, each of which uses a different roadmap. Note that self-directed work groups and management teams employ different roadmaps that aren't included here.

## *Roadmap types*

| Type | Purpose | Main roadmap actions |
|---|---|---|
| **Task team** | Implement a specific, short-term action | Plan approach to assignment<br>Implement action steps<br>Check progress and adjust accordingly<br>Report completion |
| **Problem solving** | Eradicate an undesirable, unpredictable, unworkable situation | Analyse recurring symptoms<br>Correct underlying troubles<br>Find and eliminate the root cause |
| **Process improvement** | Optimise results and control a specific, stable process that's working | Improve productivity and yield<br>Increase customer satisfaction<br>Reduce waste<br>Standardise methods<br>Control and stabilise the process |
| **New product/ process** | Develop and introduce a new product or process | Do research and benchmark technology<br>Examine methods and consider options<br>Design or re-engineer process<br>Plan and conduct experiments<br>Pilot, expand and standardise process |

A brief description of each roadmap follows. The first roadmap has the narrowest scope and, all other things being equal, will produce the quickest results, but considering your ultimate goals, is task implementation enough? Maybe the patience for a longer-term approach will provide greater pay-off eventually.

## Task/implementation team roadmap

**Step 1. Contract**
*Actions*
- Clarify scope and detail of task assignment
- Negotiate success measures with sponsor
- Establish ground rules and workable procedures
- Determine methods for meetings and minutes

**Step 2. Plan**
*Actions*
- Outline an action plan based on the task assignment
- Formulate sequence of actions and work schedule
- Break down task into milestones with defined reports

**Step 3. Do**
*Actions*
- Do what was planned
- Implement action steps

**Step 4. Check**
*Actions*
- Review progress and report accomplishments
- Assess interim results against plan

**Step 5. Next Step**
*Actions*
- Adjust plan if necessary
- Return to 3 and do the next step

**Step 6. Final Report**
*Actions*
- Document process and results
- Plan final report and conduct final presentation
- Disband or reform

# Problem-solving roadmap

### Step 1. Organise and Plan
*Actions*
- Recruit and train team members
- Define mission, team charter and master plans
- Establish meeting mechanics and build the team

### Step 2. Describe
*Actions*
- Define desired goals and customer requirements
- Map existing process and collect data to localise troubles
- Write problem statement

### Step 3. Identify Root Cause
*Actions*
- Collect and analyse data to define causes
- Examine the chain of events leading to the problem
- Brainstorm and evaluate all contributing forces
- Conduct experiments to find variables

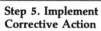

### Step 4. Decide Solution
*Actions*
- Brainstorm strategies to resolve the cause
- Compare and combine workable alternatives
- Decide on an approach all stakeholders can support

### Step 5. Implement Corrective Action
*Actions*
- Identify actions to implement the chosen strategy
- Organise steps into logical and efficient sequence
- Implement corrective action plan and verify success

### Step 6. Improve System
*Actions*
- Set up procedures to prevent future occurrences
- Document, standardise and communicate adjustments
- Design and conduct operator training
- Recommend improvements to the overall operation

### Step 7. Wrap-Up
*Actions*
- Document and present lessons learned
- Review, recognise and reward team members
- Recharter team or reassign team members

# Process improvement roadmap

### Step 1. Organise and Plan
*Actions*
- Recruit and train team members
- Define mission, team charter and master plans
- Establish meeting mechanics and build the team

### Step 2. Define Customer Satisfaction
*Actions*
- Identify internal and external customers
- Determine satisfaction levels and unsatisfied expectations
- Define ways to measure future customer satisfaction

### Step 4. Identify Process Measurements
*Actions*
- Identify variables that determine process success
- Develop new ways and means to measure new variables
- Validate that measurements are reliable and repeatable

### Step 3. Describe Process
*Actions*
- Determine and document each process step
- Define inputs and outputs for each process step
- Map a flowchart from this information

### Step 5. Measure Process
*Actions*
- Monitor process variables to baseline levels
- Collect, analyse and chart statistical process data
- Identify crucial improvement areas by identifying gaps

### Step 6. Improve Process
*Actions*
- Examine materials, methods, equipment and human factors to identify negative influences on the process
- Suggest and test alternative steps
- Activate an improvement plan to eliminate instabilities

### Step 7. Assess Progress
*Actions*
- Assess how well process improvements are working
- Document new standard operating procedures
- Conduct operator training on the improved process
- Develop a control system to maintain improvements

### Step 8. Wrap-Up
*Actions*
- Document and present lessons learned
- Review, recognise and reward team members
- Recharter team or reassign team members

# New product/process roadmap

### Step 1. Organise and Plan
*Actions*
- Recruit and train team members
- Define mission, team charter and master plans
- Establish meeting mechanics and build the team

### Step 2. New Product/Process
*Actions*
- Assess existing methods
- Benchmark similar processes and products
- Investigate new technology and brainstorm ideas

### Step 3. Feasibility Analysis
*Actions*
- Rank options and evaluate workability, cost and risk
- Re-engineer workable methods
- Experiment, build prototype and test steps

### Step 4. Approve
*Actions*
- Draft workable procedures and specifications
- Research market and define budget
- Document and present business case

### Step 5. Pilot
*Actions*
- Pilot new product/process
- Study results and refine methods
- Standardise product/process

### Step 6. Expand
*Actions*
- Buy equipment and establish permanent facilities
- Hire and train operators

### Step 7. Improve Process
*Actions*
- Continuously measure results
- Solve problems and reinforce improvements
- Manage trends and optimise processes

### Step 8. Wrap-Up
*Actions*
- Document and present lessons learned
- Review, recognise and reward team members
- Recharter team or reassign team members

*Exercise*
## Team briefing
1. Review the requirements you established for your case study team. Assuming you're the team sponsor, define the minimum sense of direction you would provide using the MRDC formula. (If none of the generic roadmaps fit, design your own.)

**Mission**

_____

_____

_____

**Roadmap choice**

_____

_____

_____

**Deliverables**

_____

_____

_____

**Constraints**

_____

_____

_____

2. Plan an agenda to brief the team so that they would start off with essential information.

_____

_____

_____

## Master planning

Teams need a simple way to overcome the natural tendency to work at cross purposes typical of most people with different personalities, backgrounds and styles. With good plans developed in common, teams are much more likely to:

- Stay focused on priorities
- Support a unified approach
- Coordinate action to avoid inefficiency
- Measure progress and maintain accountability.

Although plans, once implemented, may need to be refocused, teams gain knowledge and control through planning which allows them to adjust their path midstream when needed.

A master plan keeps teams focused and forces them to measure short-term progress. The three stages form a strategic plan.

| Phase | Contents | Methods |
|---|---|---|
| **Team charter** | General direction that identifies critical issues needing work | • Organisational goals<br>• Business strategies |
| **Master plans** | Milestones for each roadmap step with deadlines | • Long-range project plans<br>• Objectives and deliverables |
| **Action plans** | Specific work targets that define who will do what by when | • Short-range plans<br>• Team work plans |

The team roadmap makes it easy to establish two or three milestones for each roadmap step. That's the best way to develop a master plan. A specimen master plan is set out on pages 51–52.

## *Specimen Master Plan*

| Step | Milestones |
|------|-----------|
| **1. Organise and plan** | • Get team sponsor sign-off on complete mission, team charter and master plan by week 1<br>• Publish ground rules and meeting mechanics to maximise team efficiency by week 2 |
| **2. New Process** | • Issue a report that measures similar distribution processes used in related industries by week 5<br>• Get Team Steering Council commitment on preferred product distribution scheme by week 6 |
| **3. Feasibility Analysis** | • Document proposed distribution scheme including process step description, flowchart and specifications by week 7<br>• Locate and secure letter of intent from qualified outside manufacturers' representatives by week 9<br>• Publish cost analysis comparing internal versus external distribution scheme by week 10 |
| **4. Approve** | • Present business case to all internal stakeholders and secure approval of proposed distribution scheme from top management by week 12 |
| **5. Pilot** | • Pilot new product distribution process by week 14<br>• Standardise distribution process through continuous improvement and publish working procedures by week 18 |

| Step | Milestones |
|------|-----------|
| 6. Expand | • Monitor the interaction between affected departments using weekly production charts as deliveries expand from week 18 until 26 |
| 7. Improve Process | • Solve all distribution problems that arise within one week<br>• Run experiments to optimise the efficiency of forecasting and distribution processes until the returns from improvements diminish to minimal levels |
| 8. Wrap-Up | • Report lessons learned at a final Team Steering Council presentation by week 36<br>• Reassign team members to new teams that can benefit from their experience. |

## How to plan

If you ask most teams to brainstorm what they need to do, everything will tumble out, including mission, goals, inputs, outputs, war stories, actions, complaints, objectives, past failures. It won't look anything like the diagram on page 53 that shows an organised master under the umbrella of the team charter. But if you get the team to arrange and group their answers under the appropriate roadmap steps, order appears quickly.

If the team's brainstorming is typical, they may have 20 or 30 actions listed under each roadmap step. With further thought and analysis they could categorise each roadmap step's actions under two or three major accomplishments or deliverables.

To speed both planning and implementation, you need the team to distinguish inputs from outputs and start thinking in terms of milestones. Milestones are mid-range targets that break a large task into smaller but challenging chunks of output. A team uses them to pace itself, show how far it has to

# Team Charter

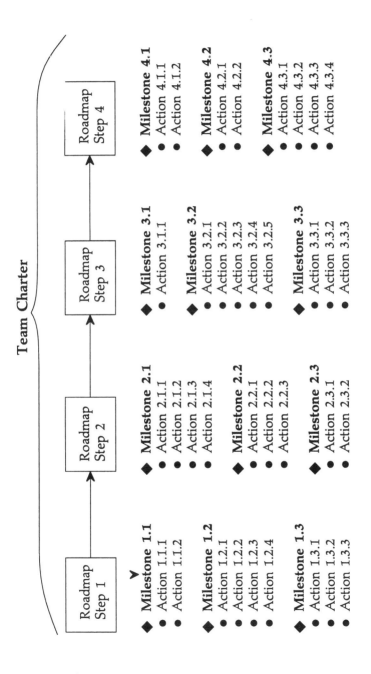

| Roadmap Step 1 | Roadmap Step 2 | Roadmap Step 3 | Roadmap Step 4 |
|---|---|---|---|

**Milestone 1.1**
- Action 1.1.1
- Action 1.1.2

**Milestone 1.2**
- Action 1.2.1
- Action 1.2.2
- Action 1.2.3
- Action 1.2.4

**Milestone 1.3**
- Action 1.3.1
- Action 1.3.2
- Action 1.3.3

**Milestone 2.1**
- Action 2.1.1
- Action 2.1.2
- Action 2.1.3
- Action 2.1.4

**Milestone 2.2**
- Action 2.2.1
- Action 2.2.2
- Action 2.2.3

**Milestone 2.3**
- Action 2.3.1
- Action 2.3.2

**Milestone 3.1**
- Action 3.1.1

**Milestone 3.2**
- Action 3.2.1
- Action 3.2.2
- Action 3.2.3
- Action 3.2.4
- Action 3.2.5

**Milestone 3.3**
- Action 3.3.1
- Action 3.3.2
- Action 3.3.3

**Milestone 4.1**
- Action 4.1.1
- Action 4.1.2

**Milestone 4.2**
- Action 4.2.1
- Action 4.2.2

**Milestone 4.3**
- Action 4.3.1
- Action 4.3.2
- Action 4.3.3
- Action 4.3.4

go and create a sense of progress. Once the categories under each roadmap step are clear, they get turned into milestones by using the same SMART Worksheet we used for deliverables on page 25.

## Master planning flowchart

The following flowchart describes this process in more detail.

1. Select or design the appropriate roadmap during team charter development.
2. Decide if you will develop milestones for roadmap steps separately or all at once.
3. Brainstorm major outcomes and critical deliverables needed to accomplish the whole plan or roadmap step.
4. Evaluate the list, identify priority deliverables and select one to three per step to serve as milestones.
5. Define each milestone as a SMART objective (specific, measurable, agreed, result-oriented and time-bound).
6. Adjust milestones by planning for contingencies, training, public relations and recognition.
7. Repeat the above for other roadmap steps or attach milestones to appropriate roadmap steps.
8. Establish a schedule by correlating milestone timeframes and charter deliverables.
9. Rewrite your plan into one clear document and map out a project tracking diagram.

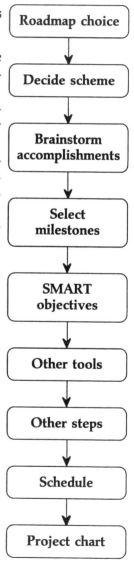

*Exercise*
**Master planning**
1. Review your case study team's mission, charter components and roadmap choice.
2. Use the roadmap descriptions to brainstorm accomplishments for each step. Record your ideas on the Master Planning Worksheet.
3. Categorise, combine, cut and edit your list to give you the fewest major accomplishments necessary to complete each roadmap step.
4. Refine initial ideas into discrete milestones with the SMART Worksheet.

### *Master Planning Worksheet*

| Roadmap step | | SMART milestones |
|---|---|---|
| | 1. | |
| | 2. | |
| | 3. | |
| | 4. | |
| | 5. | |
| | 6. | |
| | 7. | |
| | 8. | |

**Presenting the plan**
Team presentations are a great opportunity to accelerate growth or kill empowerment. Part of the team deal includes doing everything possible to see that they succeed. Here are some presentation ground rules for the team sponsor to keep the team on course:

- Don't drop in uninvited.
- Follow the team's meeting ground rules.
- Give positive reinforcement whenever and wherever possible.
- Search for things to agree with.
- Give advice when the team needs and wants coaching.
- Be flexible in adjusting plans and renegotiating the team's charter.

In spite of your best efforts, if the team comes up with impractical proposals, then:

- Respond carefully.
- Find something to agree with, to say yes instead of no.
- Identify the missing information for briefing or training the team.
- Coach the team on how to make their proposals acceptable.

*Other planning tools*
This planning method takes only a few hours and can save endless false starts and delays later. While it's a good investment, you might think that, instead of planning, the team could have been working. A team should make only plans that will help it to stabilise and speed progress, but remember the basic rule of architecture: form follows function. Use only those planning tools that team functions require. With that in mind, let's consider two other team functions that can become major obstacles to RTD if not addressed early: politics and motivation.

# Team public relations

Build the team's image and credibility with customers, suppliers and stakeholders and head off politics. How many great ideas go down because they weren't communicated persuasively? A team PR plan should include:

- **Deciding desired image.** How outsiders should view the team so that they'll value what is produced and support implementation.

- **Segmenting stakeholders.** Carving up outside circles of interested parties and assigning team member representatives to stay in touch.
- **Designing campaigns.** Deciding what messages to spread, what information to broadcast and how all this will happen.
- **Establishing reports.** Planning who should get team minutes and other documents how often.

Following through a team PR plan makes good business sense. The team will get valuable input to incorporate into their work. They'll keep their supporters in the loop enough to keep supplying resources. They'll discover related changes while there's still time to respond, and they'll surface key objections early enough to solve them.

**Team recognition**
The other obstacle that retards team acceleration is member motivation. If you've done your team sponsor homework, the team should be enthusiastic, but the fledgling team needs to know that you'll stay behind them. You need to convince them that management support won't dry up when another possibly lucrative pet scheme comes by.

That's where recognition comes in. People tend to repeat behaviour that's rewarded. Recognition is not just the compliments you pay them when they do something right or the bonuses or promotions they earn after the project is over.

Examine any high-performance team and you'll find that they party often, celebrate all successes and have lots of fun together. And this doesn't slow them down. On the contrary, the climate that's created fuels acceleration.

For RTD to work, you need a motivational system that's simple to operate, consistent and fair, routinely practised instead of forgotten, frequent enough to reward small wins, based on team achievement and under the team's control. How's that last one for truly practising empowerment?

## How to do it

Try the following process. Ask the team to plan the rewards they'll earn when delivering on their promises. Give them guidelines such as:

√ At the accomplishment of defined milestones or special effort, team members will be recognised with one of the following awards worth £15:

- Lunch
- Engraved trinket (key chain, mouse pad)
- Cinema or theatre tickets
- Team T-shirt, tie or scarf

√ At the accomplishment of major team goals, all team members will be recognised with one or more of the following awards worth £15–£75:

- Dinner and sporting event for two
- Golf umbrella.
- Sweatshirt/gift certificate.

To qualify, a team submits its master plan with defined rewards for its planned milestones. Funding for these rewards gets built into the budget. Management can set controls to ensure the goodies are affordable, and the team is guaranteed they won't be forgotten.

This reward system skirts the larger issue of how team contributions get reflected in promotions and performance reviews. You'll encourage team-building by shifting incentives throughout your organisation from individual to collective.

# CHAPTER 3
# Team-Building Dynamics

## Team kick-off

Team-building can include:

- Joint planning
- Interactive training sessions
- Consensus decision-making
- Motivation and incentive programmes
- Reorganising around self-directed work
- Developing cross-functional partnerships
- Experiential events
- Group problem-solving and conflict resolution
- Getting to know one another through games and social events.

When we started, we reviewed the stages of team development — forming, storming and norming — that lead to performing. Now we delve more into this progression and discover how to accelerate team progress. Remember, these stages are natural. We can do only so much to hasten each team member's ability to adjust, accept, learn, trust and cooperate, but we'll learn how to use tools that enhance team-building and how to avoid pitfalls that impede development.

We're studying team-building, the third stage of the team lifecycle, after the organising stage. In reality, they should happen concurrently. Give team members the freedom to do things their own way during briefing, chartering and planning, and they will develop into a coordinated working unit sooner.

### The forming stage
'Forming' stage teams tend to be:

- Unclear and uncertain about what to do and how to behave
- Polite and quiet with cautious participation
- Unfamiliar, tentative, hesitant, anxious or suspicious
- Interested only superficially, with little in-depth listening
- Worried about making a contribution and concerned about getting hurt
- Ambivalent but dependent on the team leader or dominant personality
- Uncommitted with little attachment and little work accomplished.

Because these characteristics are human nature, there's no guarantee that a forming team will start off on the right foot. You won't break any RTD records if you have to abort because few members show up for meetings, no one knows what to do or everyone argues.

The following table suggests four categories of tool to help form a team: brief them, encourage them to bond into a cohesive unit, involve them wherever possible and empower them as much as they're ready for.

### Accelerating forming stage team-building
*Briefing*

- Hold a kick-off briefing.
- Give full background information.
- Answer all questions forthrightly.
- Create a clear-cut sense of direction.
- Present team mission, goals and requirements.
- Identify outputs and deliverables needed from the team.
- Define tasks, responsibilities and individual contributions.
- Provide training on team roles, tools and basic processes.

*Bonding*

- Make team members feel welcome and needed.
- Develop relationships to unify team members.
- Help the team to learn about one another's background and skills.
- Schedule a tour of each team member's work area.
- Teach them to work through each other's personal style.
- Establish ground rules to develop common ground.
- Ensure that personal goals will be achieved through the team.
- Encourage team members to connect.
- Build mutual trust between members, team and management.

*Involvement*

- Use warm-up exercises to focus energy.
- Challenge the team to get involved.
- Introduce activities to demonstrate cooperation.
- Cultivate participation with communication.
- Encourage creativity, accept feedback and capture all input.
- Generate new ideas about team charter and plans.
- Brainstorm problems and their causes.
- Address initial concerns honestly and flexibly.

*Empowerment*

- Let the team finalise its charter.
- Have the team develop a master plan.
- Let the team run meetings as soon as possible.
- Guide the team to distribute its workload.
- Identify expectations to uncover common goals.
- Encourage and facilitate consensus decision making.
- Delegate to the team decisions about priorities.
- Help the team to resolve conflicts on its own.

You don't have to do everything on this list – use only the tools that the team need for rapid growth. Maybe you'll be lucky and find that the human side of team formation happens on its own during organising activities, but in case it doesn't, we will look at the one group we've ignored so far: bonding.

## Bonding teams

To function as a team, individuals must bond into a cohesive unit. The ties that members develop start with personal contact, grow into stronger connections as team members work together and ultimately create a solid union when trust and respect develop.

Sometimes just throwing all the right pieces together isn't enough. Team members often have serious questions such as:

- Will I be accepted and needed?
- What will I have to give up if I join?
- Who will be in charge and what power will they hold?
- Will my voice be heard?
- Will my contributions be valued?
- How concerned is the team for my welfare?

If these questions aren't answered, cooperative relationships won't form.

To ensure that the right answers are found quickly, many team builders allocate time early for team bonding. We'll discuss four bonding methods that have the highest leverage on team speed — communication, ground rules, training and trust building.

## Team communication guidelines

Communication is vital for team mates to work together smoothly. Gaps, breakdowns, misunderstandings and unwillingness to open up may do more to slow teams down than any other internal factor.

Include communication skill-building exercises in initial training. Encourage teams to include these dos and don'ts in their ground rules, and then give them feedback and coaching to help them find new ways of behaving.

| Do | Don't |
|---|---|
| • Organise thoughts<br>• Assert your opinion<br>• Listen actively<br>• Be open<br>• Respond | • Clutter thoughts<br>• Be aggressive<br>• Block others<br>• Close your mind<br>• Resist |

## Team ground rules

When a team first gets together, neither new team mates nor seasoned veterans automatically know the best way to act towards one another. The smart thing to do is to develop a tailored set of team ground rules, which are statements of basic values that a team establishes to serve as behavioural guidelines so that individual team members know how to interact and support one another. You can use them to standardise procedure, time management, work assignments, logistics, preparation, discussion, creativity, reporting, respect, courtesy and problem-solving. The following worksheet helps.

### *Team Ground Rules Worksheet*

| Ground rule category | Team ground rules |
|---|---|
| **Respect.** How team members should work together, treat one another; handle rank, equality, confidentiality, recognition and courtesy. | |
| **Responsibility.** How team members will delegate assignments and distribute action items. | |
| **Procedures.** How the team will plan, record and report its work; set priorities, handle changes and make decisions. | |

| Ground rule category | Team ground rules |
|---|---|
| **Discussion.** How team members will participate, communicate and give feedback. | |
| **Differences.** How the team will handle disagreements and criticism. | |
| **Schedule.** When the team will meet and for how long; how it will regulate attendance, promptness, breaks and interruptions. | |
| **Meetings.** How the team will prepare agendas, judge a quorum, respond to absences and replacements, handle interruptions and tangents, document minutes. | |
| **Work management.** How the team will manage its project, monitor progress, stay on track, report success and problems, represent status to outsiders. | |
| **Non-team behaviour.** How the team will improve poor motivation or attitude, ignored action items, smoking, inappropriate behaviour or language. | |

A new team should define its most obvious ground rules as soon as possible. If the team follows the rules of brainstorming, lots of ideas, good and bad, will surface. The team should go over the list and decide on the minimum essentials. Don't expect a team to cover every conceivable issue at the start. Just publish the list and post it on a chart for reference during all team meetings.

Good ground rules are clear, consistent, agreed to, reinforced and followed, so encourage everyone to take them seriously. As the team progresses, they can revise them in response to unexpected situations, problems or awareness of what's necessary for success. Keep the list visible. If ground rules work as planned, the team's connections will get stronger as they take charge of their own relationships.

# Team training

A powerful bonding experience often happens in team training. When new teams work together, they learn what they need to do, how to operate in unison and how to use new team tools. They discover how to work better together than they would have separately. Team training involves:

- **Team building skills.** How to define roles, share responsibility, encourage participation, structure cooperation, establish ground rules, conduct warm-ups and work through differences.
- **Organising skills.** How to develop a mission statement, team charter, roadmap, master plan, short-range action plans, budgets, schedule and PR plans.
- **People skills.** How to listen actively, communicate clearly, lead, coach, train, negotiate, present to groups, resolve conflicts and troubleshoot problems.
- **Meeting skills.** How to organise meetings, plan agendas, moderate discussion, generate ideas, make consensus decisions, close discussions and establish action items.
- **Supporting tools.** How to use tools to collect and analyse data, find root causes, solve problems, use statistical process controls, read charts, design roadmaps and make continuous improvements.
- **Work and project management.** How to coordinate efforts, measure quality, monitor progress, interface with

stakeholders, manage finances, control costs and document actions.

- **Technical skills.** How to understand the systems, conduct the functions, operate the equipment and improve the processes the team is responsible for, including extensive cross-training on each other's jobs.

Depending on team charter and planned investment in team performance level, decide which of these topics to include in your team's training.

**Team kick-off training**
The best way to kick off an RTD team is at an off-site retreat. This way, you can address everything at once and rapid deployment of a soon-to-be high-performance team becomes possible. When a retreat isn't practical, come as close to that ideal as you can. Schedule longer and more frequent initial team meetings that include one or two hours of training each. Remember, a slow start can dramatically slow down urgently needed team results.

One team orchestrated their kick-off training at an initial off-site retreat and several follow-up meetings, as follows:

| Led by Team ... | Topic | Process |
|---|---|---|
| Facilitator | Orientation to team process | *Presentation* |
| Leader | Team warm-up to get to know one another | *Discussion* |
| Sponsor | Mission and background | *Presentation* |
| Facilitator | Team concepts and methods | *Training* |
| Leader | Setting ground rules | *Discussion* |
| Facilitator | Team meeting processes | *Training* |

| Led by Team ... | Topic | Process |
|---|---|---|
| Leader | Choosing roles and rotation scheme | *Discussion* |
| Facilitator | Consensus decision making | *Training* |
| Leader | Resolve initial issues and conflicts | *Consensus* |
| Facilitator | Team charter components | *Training* |
| Leader | Team charter development | *Consensus* |
| Sponsor | Team charter proposal | *Negotiation* |
| Facilitator | Team roadmap and planning tools | *Training* |
| Leader | Develop master, PR and recognition plan | *Consensus* |
| Sponsor | Master plan proposal | *Negotiation* |
| Facilitator | Data collection, problem-solving, quality tools | *Training* |
| Leader | Action plans to accomplish first milestone | *Consensus* |

## Just-in-time team training

The recommended agenda for team kick-off training just scratches the surface of what high-performance teams eventually master. Of course, it's impractical to teach a forming team everything they'll need to know all at once. Even if you could teach everything at one sitting, most people would forget what they don't apply immediately. So reality presents us with another critical question: How do you do other important training while the team gets some work done?

Just-in-time training is the solution. Start the team with as much intensive training as possible. Since you'll never cover everything needed, remain alert to training gaps that occur. Respond with short sessions appropriate to what the team is working on. Midstream intensive workshops help, but 5- to 30-minute modules at the right time can meet 80 per cent of the team's remaining training needs.

Think how much faster you could deploy teams if everyone in your organisation were trained on team tools and mechanics. If you're planning more teams or an entire team environment, maybe you should refocus from immediate results and consider training time and money as a long-term investment.

### How to break mutual trust

Mutual trust between team and management is essential for high-performance teamwork. Without it, teams won't function at all. With it, the pace of team growth is sometimes startling. If:

- defensiveness
- fear of failure
- ulterior motives
- hidden agendas
- self-serving behaviour
- strong emotional reactions
- embarrassment in exposing feelings
- unwillingness to admit problems
- guarded speech
- judging and overt button pushing exist

then you must include building mutual trust as a team-development target.

Trust builds gradually and breaks suddenly. Once broken, it isn't easily recovered, if ever. Here are some ways which cause trust to plummet:

- Changing the rules of the game midstream
- Holding information back
- Continuously looking over the team's shoulder
- Micromanaging and oversupervising
- Frequently criticising team actions
- Playing politics with team resources and proposals

- Always playing devil's advocate on team proposals
- Ignoring team minutes and reports
- Taking no action on team proposals
- Not providing promised resources and rewards
- Rewarding non-team players.

## How to build mutual trust

On the plus side, the following elements contribute to building trust:

- **Honesty.** Truth with integrity and without exaggerations or lies
- **Openness.** Willingness to listen fully and share all ideas and feelings
- **Consistency.** Predictable responses and stable principles
- **Respect.** Treating all people with dignity, equality and fairness
- **Promises.** Team members who always keep their word without fail.

*Trust-building strategies*

Use the following seven strategies to build team trust.

1. Allocate time for team-building activities
2. Provide ample autonomy
3. Encourage risk taking
4. Let communication run its full course
5. Encourage and act on feedback from the team
6. Help them to feel secure in admitting mistakes
7. Help the team to become self-correcting.

*Exercise*

## Team training

Consider the slate you established for your case study team, the experience of the proposed members and its proposed team charter.

1. Which team-building activities would help to bond this team rapidly?

_____

_____

_____

**2.** Which ground rules will be essential for this team?

_____

_____

_____

**3.** Plan an agenda for initial team training including any items above.

_____

_____

_____

**4.** Decide how to schedule the team's kick-off (retreat, location, frequent meetings, timing).

_____

_____

_____

## Handling team differences

To succeed, a team must remain focused on its overall mission. Shared goals and individual commitment to the larger good are essential. Everyone must learn to trust one another enough to work together. Unfortunately, these requirements don't automatically accompany the decision to form a team.

### Storming symptoms
If individuals' issues take higher priority than collective success, the project will probably fail. The team will be distracted, cooperation become difficult, morale drop, time be

lost, and progress may be halted. This can happen at any point of team growth but is widespread during the storming stage, which may include the following symptoms:

- Overt challenges and disagreements
- Demands about personal concerns and independence
- Criticism, attacks and strong emotional reactions
- Jealousy and distrust of team members
- Hidden agendas, turf politics, cliques and splinter groups
- Testing leadership and control
- Stress, confusion and distractions
- Work accomplished only in fits and starts.

### Why differences?
People are different, and since teams work hard to draw out everyone's ideas and feelings, these differences emerge quickly. Even in the most seasoned groups, conflicting positions between team members are natural and occur all the time, but you can spot an immature team by noticing its majority of unwilling, uncommitted or uncooperative members.

### Disruptions
To prevent natural differences from disrupting team progress, good team leaders try to resolve individual issues outside meetings. When friction is ignored or handled poorly, the team gets distracted from its work. Disruptions appear when the team feels uncomfortable, storms instead of works, gets off track, wastes time or has its progress impeded. When handled constructively, differences stimulate creativity.

When disruptions aren't handled early enough, conflict appears as total communication breakdowns, strong emotional reactions, team members leaving, personality clashes or out of control meetings.

Most teams expect the team leader to handle disruptions because the effect is cumulative. The more it happens, the worse it gets. Conflict can be a learning experience too, but it's time consuming and energy draining. The more you can prevent conflict from happening, the faster your team will progress.

## Alternatives for handling differences
When you accept that a team needs to learn to handle these troubles professionally, what do you do? Reacting negatively to a difference of opinion results in encouraging conformity, hampering creativity, discarding new ideas and invalidating the consensus concept.

## Storming recommendations
Here are some principles your team could use to get through storming the best and fastest way.

| Principle | Suggested application |
|-----------|----------------------|
| **Welcome differences** | • Encourage frank expression of personal concerns<br>• Accept all input and respect all team members' positions<br>• Find something positive in every divergent view<br>• Treat all feelings and opinions as belonging to the whole team<br>• Incorporate and integrate all statements into team discussion<br>• Document all comments in team notes and minutes<br>• Recognise, don't avoid, frustrated team members<br>• Ensure anyone can speak openly without repercussions |
| **React positively** | • Encourage team members to air differences<br>• Be positive and constructive in the face of conflict<br>• Patiently but assertively moderate discussion<br>• Honour personal needs and advocate individual welfare |

| Principle | Suggested application |
|---|---|
| | • Work to fix the problem, not the blame<br>• Maintain and enhance individual self-esteem |
| **Use empathy** | • Listen actively and as an ally<br>• Acknowledge understanding before presenting alternatives<br>• Ensure everyone feels their voice is heard<br>• Focus on others' ideas and feelings<br>• Give team mates the benefit of the doubt<br>• Try to see things from the other person's viewpoint<br>• Relate similar situations that you've observed |
| **Use positive feedback** | • Use recognition and advice instead of criticism or punishment<br>• Use 'I' statements to avoid judging and evaluating<br>• Focus on the situation, not the person<br>• Coach by being direct, specific, assertive, firm and helpful<br>• Use your body language to show that others count<br>• Balance everything you do with positive reinforcement |
| **Confront problems** | • Explore differences by discussing all sides openly<br>• Prevent worse problems by acting before things get serious<br>• Find root causes, not symptoms, to find solutions<br>• When facing problems, remember: Sooner is easier<br>• Take personal responsibility whether it's your problem or not<br>• Turn all conflict situations into learning opportunities |

| Principle | Suggested application |
|---|---|
| **Negotiate solutions together** | • Try to negotiate win–wins by collaborating on solutions<br>• Encourage team mates to solve one another's problems<br>• Facilitate group decision making by seeking consensus<br>• Adjust mission, charter, roles and responsibilities as needed |

## How to negotiate differences

Even if your team's ground rules reflect good dialogue and positive feedback, they may still run into issues that divide them. What do you do about such impasses? Negotiate. Negotiation means exchanging views to reach agreement. Teamwork demands a win–win from every disagreement, where both sides are fair to each other and walk away satisfied that each has gained something.

If you had to solve a team mate's problem, you wouldn't recommend something you couldn't live with, would you? That's the team way of negotiating differences, as presented below.

*Presentations*
Each presents their reality while the other listens, acknowledges and interrupts only to clarify understanding. Recording comments at this point is useful. A discussion moderator may help to ensure that communication works.

*Agreements*
Both sides find, discuss and list areas of agreement, common goals, interests, values and views. Don't cut this step short. Agreements are usually the key to resolving differences.

*Differences*
Identify issues of disagreement that interfere with complete agreement. Narrow the key differences to the top one or two, then discuss them in depth to understand opposing views and finally define the exact problem.

*Negotiation*
Discuss ways to resolve the differences, with each party trying to solve the other's problem. Consider alternatives and evaluate strategies until you find a mutually acceptable solution for each issue. End only when you agree on implementation.

This sequence lets each party feel heard, concentrates on common goals first and uses a constructive approach to bridge any remaining gaps. If you follow this agenda, you'll be miles ahead while other teams are still arguing.

*Exercise*
**Negotiating differences**
The following exercise uses this approach for negotiating differences.

1. Select a likely conflict between two members of your case study team.
2. Using the Win–Win Worksheet, define the two sides of the issue.
3. Examine agreements and unwritten contracts that the two share.
4. Define one or two pivotal differences that separate them.
5. Brainstorm several win–win solutions. Come up with at least three, since, in the real world, the first answer doesn't always work.

## *Win–Win Worksheet*

| What are the situations and interests of the two parties (goals, needs, purposes, approaches, data, positions on issues)? | |
|---|---|
| | |

| What do the two parties have in common? |
|---|
| |

| On what do the two parties differ? |
|---|
| |

| What potential options might satisfy both parties? |
|---|
| |

# CHAPTER 4
# Accelerating Teamwork

## Increasing your team's pace

With any luck, your team is approaching the norming stage after just a few days or weeks. Indicators of a norming team include:

- Enough stability to progress and get itself out of trouble
- Understanding team boundaries and emerging behavioural norms
- Shifting attention from blaming one another to solving problems
- Confidence to act like a team instead of individuals
- More consensus on issues and easier resolution of differences
- Moderate and increasing amounts of work accomplished.

Here are some guidelines for improving mid-project teamwork.

- Adjust roles, goals, ground rules and processes
- Reaffirm procedures by working through rough spots
- Encourage improvements by recognising progress
- Stretch the team
- Let them find answers to stresses on their own sooner rather than later
- Delegate functions as soon as the team can handle them

## Team action plans
Teamwork requires the coordinated effort of multiple minds, mouths and hands. To accomplish this, the fastest teams plan their work and then work their plan. They focus on making progress one step at a time together, and they need the type of short-term tactics that an action plan defines.

An action plan is a series of specific tasks that a team works out in advance to reach a milestone. In their simplest form, action plans dictate who will do what, when. In their most detailed form, they contain:

- Activities
- Delegated responsibilities
- PR, training and recognition plans
- Personnel
- Solutions to human factors
- Resources
- Control systems.

## Team delegation
Your team should build action plans to share responsibility, distribute workload and use everyone's talents, but some teams try to do everything together. Not only does this create unnecessary work, it's frustrating.

## Consensus defined
The speed of team progress depends on how quickly and effectively members pool information and backgrounds and agree on goals, plans and actions. This effort can be subverted when everyone has a different view, strong-willed people won't give in, some dominate conversation, easy-going members avoid conflict, members won't express an opinion or some change the subject. Often the majority or the most powerful person decides.

Can rapid team deployment work this way and reach high performance? No, not if open participation is limited, minority views are rejected or team member input is ignored. Does this mean that every team discussion must result in an identical, unanimous view? Let's hope not.

The solution is to make key team decisions by consensus, which means by *general agreement*. Consensus is not usually one person's idea, nor is it everyone's first choice. Consensus is a decision reflecting the collective thinking of a team that all team members participate in developing, understand, believe is workable and will support. A consensus position is one that merges everyone's views.

*How to reach consensus*
To reach consensus, every team member must participate fully, be open-minded, offer solutions to differences and seek agreement. Cutting off discussion by asking for a majority vote will work against this process. Disagreements must be confronted and explored until win–win solutions are found.

| **Generate Ideas** | | |
|---|---|---|
| • Brainstorm ideas | • Build participation | |
| • Stimulate discussion | • Encourage creativity | |
| **Process Ideas** | | |
| • Clarify ideas | • Guide discussion | • Understand one another |
| **Make Decisions** | | |
| • Prioritise ideas | • Build consensus | |
| • Close discussion | • Generate agreement | |

This approach to making team decisions is open and fair, but it requires more time and skilled facilitation to complete group discussion. Don't expect rapid consensus on every issue. Early in a team's growth, choose where universal support is vital, and use a quicker decision scheme for less vital situations. For example, consider using consensus to establish the team's charter, ground rules and project plans. Team conflicts should usually be resolved by consensus. Consider using a faster decision-making method such as majority voting or team leader choice for issues that may be non-critical, including meeting location, action item assignment and exact wording of minutes.

## Effective meetings

Plan your meeting and meet according to plan. If you don't get organised for an hour's personal work and operate only at 25 per cent strength, you've wasted 45 minutes. If the same disorganisation happens with a team of eight, you've wasted six hours. An effective team meeting includes:

- clear goals
- published agenda
- prepared members and speakers
- full but focused participation
- time control
- public recording of ideas
- group process management
- closure.

High-performance teams demonstrate equal input, balanced participation and shared leadership. They raise thorny issues, debate them heatedly and digest consensus out of confusion – and they do it in unison, getting the best out of one another without wasting time or ignoring input.

### *Meeting hats*

How do they do it? Practice helps, but they have also worked out a scheme to share meeting control and decision making. Although there's no mandatory arrangement, here's one way to rotate tasks.

- **Meeting chair.** Organises the agenda, calls the meeting to order, announces items, assigns roles, asks for closure (usually the team leader).
- **Discussion moderator.** Asks questions, balances participation, regulates dominators, keeps the group on track.
- **Timekeeper.** Notes time frames, watches the clock, announces time remaining and deadlines.
- **Recorder.** Itemises points on flipcharts and takes notes.

The division of labour works well this way, but do whatever works for your group. Just make sure each shares the burden.

# Project management

Many team sponsors think empowerment means to leave the team alone; however, abdicating total control ultimately backfires. Healthy teams grow a sense of responsibility to the organisation, respond to being held accountable and feed on a challenge. So a key rule of accelerating progress is to stay in touch.

Managing a team project occurs in five distinct stages:

1. **Start-up.** Ensure plans are documented and reduced to small, measurable chunks, ensuring that first steps succeed.
2. **Monitoring progress.** Keep the team on track by establishing and monitoring checkpoints, requiring action plans for new milestones and adjusting master plans as needed.
3. **Reinforcement.** Recognise even the smallest wins; remind the team of commitments and provide needed coaching, training and rewards.
4. **Troubleshooting.** Investigate troubles quickly, conduct problem-solving meetings, encourage the team to take swift correction or propose changes.
5. **Close down.** Recognise finished steps, complete loose ends, document progress and lessons learned, publicise results and celebrate success.

## Monitoring

A team should keep track of what it does and how it succeeds so it can reinforce what works or correct what doesn't before it's too late. A good monitoring system should be:

- Quick and easy to operate
- Reliable and accurate
- Frequent enough to show positive and negative trends
- Based on team goals and objectives
- Reviewed soon enough to take action.

What should a team monitor to improve its operations? What should a team sponsor monitor to ensure team accountability? Remember the basic rule of monitoring – that which gets measured, gets done.

Any team with a decent charter and master plan will have defined goals, key deliverables and SMART objectives based on customer requirements. You know that you want to measure satisfaction, quality or productivity — but that's not easy, especially when teams try to measure themselves at weekly meetings.

Many people struggle with establishing performance measures to quantify team progress, which are hardest to define when you insist on scientific precision. That's really unnecessary in a continuous improvement scheme like team building. You don't need a perfect scoring system to indicate performance trend. Here are some measures you can use to track three aspects of teamwork.

*Task progress*
- Percentage of roadmap steps completed
- Number of weeks ahead or behind master schedule
- Percentage of action items completed before each meeting
- Percentage of improvements implemented.

*Meeting effectiveness*
- Number of team members attending each meeting
- Percentage of meeting time spent on team tasks rather than details or conflicts
- Range of team member participation during meetings.

*Team maturity*
- Percentage of initial training completed
- Stage of team development (forming, storming, norming)
- Score on Team Performance Rating Form (13 points on page 8).

You can probably define more specific measures tied to the team's charter. Until a team is self-sufficient, self-regulating and self-correcting, let the team facilitator judge softer dynamics such as empowerment, process awareness, commitment and consensus.

## Action register

It's easy for a team to lose track of its activities in the midst of a busy work schedule. Many teams use their minutes to document any action items established in meetings. Action items record the assignment of *who* is responsible for doing *what* by *when*. Put these on the front page of the minutes so they don't get ignored.

Some assignments take longer than the time between team meetings. If you don't review action items, they're easily forgotten. An action register is an RTD tool that can help to prevent loose ends. Here's a form for an action register and what you would list in each column.

| Priority level | Action item | Assigned to | Date due | Date complete |
| --- | --- | --- | --- | --- |
| | | | | |
| | | | | |
| | | | | |
| | | | | |
| | | | | |
| | | | | |
| | | | | |

### Team self-monitoring

When a team's future rests in the hands of others who read reports months later, little improvement occurs. That's why the best monitoring is real-time self-monitoring. To do this, high-performance teams establish checkpoints, solicit feedback and analyse their performance. Then the team can reinforce, adjust and react to what's happening sooner.

### Coaching

Leadership has its place, but if you use too much command and control with a team, you can stifle motivation, energy and commitment. On the other hand, you can't ignore a situation that could be improved. Coaching is the solution.

A coach is a mentor who advises another, provides direction, gives feedback, reinforces what works and suggests ways to improve. This is how all team players should interact. The team sponsor coaches the team and team leader about the project. The team facilitator coaches them and the team sponsor on group dynamics. The team leader coaches team members on their assignments and they coach one another and outside co-workers. When there's an opportunity to do things better and quicker, coaching works.

*Exercise*
**Accelerating teamwork**
List at least three acceleration tools to put to work with your case study team.

1._____

2._____

3._____

# Unsticking stuck teams

If your team-building has succeeded, your team has arrived at high performance. If you're not so lucky, your team may be stuck. Many teams run into a major obstacle, get distracted or never seem to get organised.

Use the Troubleshooting Tool to find your way to unstick a stuck team. The four main headings represent the key logical stages for internal problem solving. The questions within each heading suggest alternative ways to help a team diagnose a resource gap, resolve a conflict or get the team back on track.

*Troubleshooting Tool*

---

**Problem description**
1. What do you know about the problem?
2. Who is involved and how are they affected?
3. What obstacles impede what goals?
4. How do things differ from the way we want them to be?

---

**Cause analysis**
1. What forces contribute to the problem?
2. Why does the problem exist?
3. What started the chain of events that brought us here?
4. What is the root cause?

---

**Solution decision**
1. What strategies would resolve the situation?
2. How can we be sure to resolve the root cause?
3. How do the possible solutions compare to each other?
4. Which is the most workable solution to achieve our goals best?

---

**Implementation plans**
1. What actions are required to solve the problem?
2. Who needs to do what to implement the decision?
3. How long will each step take?
4. What resources are needed to implement the solution?

---

# Adjusting team membership

Sometimes, despite your best efforts, the problem lies not in the process but a person — one specific team member. In that case, start at No 1 and proceed only if needed.

1. Team members give private feedback to their team mates and the team leader about the problem.
2. The team leader coaches the team member based on existing contracts, team ground rules and common perceptions, asking for team facilitator help if necessary.
3. The team leader asks an outside authority such as the team

sponsor or the team member's immediate supervisor to clear up any misunderstandings or conflicts on issues such as time, goals or priorities.

4. The team leader conducts a group problem-solving session on the team's situation without blaming the team member.
5. The team sponsor changes the team member's status to that of consultant who doesn't attend all meetings or participate in team decisions.
6. The team member willingly agrees to leave the team.
7. Team sponsor replaces the team member.

### Incorporating new team members

Whether it's necessary to solve a problem or just because people move on, team membership won't remain stable for ever, and when the players change, team dynamics also change. You've got new personalities to adjust to and new skills to exploit.

Since high-performance teamwork grows out of the agreements forged by a developing group, even the most valuable newcomer creates a new set of problems. Should you start team-building all over again? It's unlikely that you'll have the time and support for that. Should you just hope the newcomer gets accepted eventually? That's risky for the individual and likely to slow teamwork.

Here's a programme the team leader can follow to incorporate new team members into the mainstream.

- **Contracting.** Meet the newcomer to define expectations for participation.
- **Welcome.** Publicly welcome and introduce the newcomer to the team.
- **Personal contacts.** Have each team member talk with the newcomer individually so they all get to know one another.
- **Mentor.** Appoint one team member to acquaint the newcomer with team procedures.
- **Documents.** Give the newcomer a copy of all team documents, including team charter, ground rules, plans, data, minutes and reports.
- **Brief.** Brief the newcomer on team history, ground rules, procedures, processes, charter and plans.

- **Role.** Give the newcomer a defined role to enable participation from the beginning.
- **Involve.** Ensure the discussion moderator encourages equal newcomer participation in team discussions and assignment of action items.
- **Coach.** Give the newcomer feedback to reinforce what's working and advise how to improve participation.
- **Audit.** When the newcomer is ready, ask for a personal audit of team structure and performance, scheduling a formal report including recommendations on the team agenda.

# CHAPTER 5
# Close Down

You've worked hard to build a unit that has worked harder and smarter than a group of individuals could have separately. Now their charter is complete. It's time to move on, but your team doesn't want to break up. What can you do? You have three options:

- **Extend the team's charter.** So they can have more responsibility for implementation, greater scope in their assignment or additional milestones.
- **Recharter the same group.** To tackle a new challenge with a new project.
- **Disband the team.** Redeploy the team members in jobs where they can use their talents or as the nucleus of new projects.

We've already covered the tools for the first two options. The third is the trickiest, especially if you hope to recruit motivated people to deploy future teams. Here's where the fifth stage of team development comes into play: adjourning.

### The adjourning stage
Many managers and teams don't devote the attention necessary to complete the job. There are new fires to fight and new ambitions to satisfy, so they abandon the old project and rush off to the new challenge. Still, human beings crave

and benefit from closure. To achieve it, wrap up your project effectively with these four key actions.

*1. Final report*
Don't reinvent the wheel. You need to document what your successful team did so others can benefit from your experience. Ensure the team develops a comprehensive project description, including:

- a brief summary
- the process or problem studied
- key data collected
- pivotal decisions made
- mistakes, obstacles and solutions
- technical and process lessons learned and their impact
- accomplishments
- implementation methods and status at the time of completion.

This document will serve as your organisation's primary written reference for the project. If your team has maintained a notebook of plans, data and minutes, the final report shouldn't be an impossible chore. Enter the report into a team and process history database. Whether or not the project was worthwhile, the final report will be.

*2. Final presentation*
Although your team has undoubtedly been meeting and debriefing the team sponsor right up to the end, plan a final summary presentation to close out the project. Invite senior management, stakeholders and even external customers. Prepare snazzy colour visuals and refreshments. Of course, you'll want to hand out copies of your final report.

*3. Recognition*
Recognising team member contributions is not just a nicety that management should feel obliged to do, it's the key to making rapid team deployment work in the future. Rewarded behaviour is repeated, but word gets around when manage-

ment secretly believes teamwork is an effective tool to exploit workers and get something for nothing. Money is a nice reward for good teamwork, but is not the point. Giving credit where credit is due is crucial to the team process.

Further, high-performance team members undergo tremendous personal development. Because of their joint efforts, the members of a successful team are now experts in the problem or process they studied. This work should be reflected in performance reviews and promotions, but these people are also invaluable as future team builders. Using successful team members as ambassadors not only gets the word out, it's great recognition.

Finally, because of all the trauma, stretching and long hours, management really does owe the group one last company-funded party. You know that high-performance teams have more fun and celebrate more often than other people, so make your final bash worthy of their accomplishment.

*4. Deploying results*
The previous three actions help to deploy the lessons learned to maximum advantage. However, sometimes a task force's recommendations are ignored by those with the power to improve things. Don't let your team's project results die a slow death. Instead, apply some or all of these suggestions:

- Don't let the team disband until implementation is complete or at least well underway with their guidance.
- Ensure they develop and install a continuing control system to prevent past problems from recurring.
- Distribute their final report or have it published as a technical article.
- Have them make their presentation at other facilities.
- Put key team members to work on developing training materials so their new-found expertise is never lost.
- Have them train anyone who could benefit from what they learned.
- Reassign team members as the nucleus of new teams who can profit from their experience.

- Promote team members to new jobs where they capitalise on their personal development, technical knowledge and team expertise.

# Other teamwork titles available from Kogan Page

*Achieving Goals Through Teamwork*, Manchester Open Learning, 1993

*Building a Dynamic Team*, Richard Y Chang, 1995

*Building Your Team*, Rupert Eales-White, 1995

*Creating Top Flight Teams*, Hilarie Owen, 1996

*Facilitation Skills for Team Leaders*, Donald Hackett and Charles L Martin, 1994

*Measuring Team Performance*, Richard Y Chang, Gloria E Bader and Audrey E Bloom, 1995

*Success Through Teamwork*, Richard Y Chang, 1995

*Team Decision-Making Techniques*, P Keith Kelly, 1995